JOURNEYS & BAGGAGE

a book of poems and water-colours

Poems

Margaret Leff

Water-colours

Tessa Hagity

First published in the United Kingdom by

T. Hagity

38 Twisden Road

London

NW5 1DN

ISBN 1–902613–04–X

Poems edited by Richard Bates

Designed and typeset in Frutiger by Discript Limited, London WC2N 4BN

Printed in the United Kingdom by The Cromwell Press Limited, Trowbridge, Wiltshire

Contents

To our family,

The Gitlins

A Dinghy on
Monkey Bay
(or How I learned
to sail)

A dinghy, and a sail,
Spun me off from Monkey Bay.
The wind holding fast,
Into the colours of that day.
Alone, where sky and waters meet.

At midday, winds failed.
Lolling in the bottom of my boat,
Feet up, hat down, what did I care
If the long tacks took all day.
There was time to spare on Monkey Bay.

Journeys
& baggage

Some carry too much
And hold too tight.

Some are careless.
Leaving a messy trail.

Some travel light.
Loose cannons on the deck.

Balancing though is always
A difficult act.

Castiglione della
Pescaia

Was an ancient fishing town,
Now a busy seaquay resort.
Façaded, a theatrical backdrop
Let down for the season's sun,
Where reality disappears
In a soporific daze,
And skins colour on their spit of sand,
From painful red, to darkest brown.

A silvery, glittering, shallow sea
Stretches out to a heat hazed sky,
As yet another circle is spun,
From this brilliant beach, to the sun.
At night, the buzz of diverse tongues,
Carries on the warm, lit air,
Clothes are worn to catch the eye,
By those who are drifting by.

And they who sit at open bars
Observing games the players play.
Are themselves part of the scene,
Audience to a summer holiday.

My friend Bill

A first and gentle love
Always finds space in my heart.

Sometimes I sit and think of him;
His smiling eyes, and kindly ways
Are part of my youth.

Now, he is lost to a coral reef
Held down, on the ocean floor.

In a life he loved, he lost his life.
And the caves of the sea
Now, know more than me . . .

But a part of him is always me.
That element belonging to memory.

A sea grave

Their bones steel clean,
Covered with drifting sand.

The souls of the dead
Weep in the ocean.
From deep sightless eyes,
Bubble silver tears.

As they face a sky
Of the rolling shifting seas.

The reefs
of the sea

On the bed of the sea
By a sandy reef,
Lies the city, submerged.

Waters move, drifting
As gracious winds,
Through lodges of antiquity.

Fish stream, shaded dark
Shadows, in their rhythmic world.
Companion to long-lost souls
Whose spirits search for land.

Hope

Carried on a song to the sky,
Caught in a silver spray
Soar, love and hope.

In the depth of an ocean wave,
Or moving on a cold dry wind
Lie, sadness and fear.

Each transient in time and place.

Sea spume

When hopes rise up,
Like spume from the sea,
And sunlight catches
The brilliant fall.
When all is free,
And light with grace.
That, is the age to be.

Driftlines

The commitment to time
Limits all things.

But as driftlines sway
On the ocean swell,
Fellow travellers may
Move with the current

And stay awhile
As the world tilts.

It's windy

Time is the wind
Blowing through our lives.
Sometimes gentle,
A drifting breeze
To dream and grow in.
Sometimes racing,
A tempest to our days
And wilder ways.
Sometimes cold,
A harsh reminder
Of our mortality.

Nerves

When I am not sad,
I like the darkness
Of night,
And the secrecy
Of a new day.
Otherwise, I get nervous
Of both.

A last adventure

Sometimes I want to fling
Everything away.

To start again,
Clean and free.

But, habit holds . . .
And those I love,
Thankfully, hold to me.

Today is
not my day

Today is not my day
It started out that way.
A joker in the pack
Changed a point of reference.
But time, like water held
Will quietly drain away
Into another day.

Distant music

I am lost in music
As if from an old star,
Falling from a dark sky;

I listen and muse
To the faint echo
Of distant memories.

Interpretation

Dream, deep in the night
Worlds strange as legend.
Of quick-changing mood
And vision.

Where sometimes,
Unconscious fantasy
Is more truthful than ordered days;
If emotion is interpreted
Not spectre.

Mean streets

There are places in every city
Where the streets seem racked with gloom,
And all of the days are as night.

Paper and tins blow in the wind,
Jagged glass glints up from the road.
Sly thin cats slink on their way,
Randy hounds of indeterminate breed
Cavort, to frighten the children at play.
Lifestyles trail from rubbish bins
Strewn carelessly along the road.
Open windows, filled with noise.

Growth in a street like this
Can be rackety, withered or scarred.
But there are brilliant blooms,
All the more radiant midst the blight.

Sharon's death

I see a city, dark lit:
Shifting profiles, shadows
On the streets of night.

Flashing needles,
Pumping veins,
Mucky powders.

A sweet deadly release,
And she slides to her death
From a municipal toilet seat.

As darkness steals the day,
In nightland, one shadow less
Leaps the cityscape.

Smallson,
Jack Russell

"I am a roughly ginger dog
And live in NW3.

Some say my legs
Are a little long.
Others, that they fit
Just p e r f e c t l y.

I greet my friends,
When not at home,
Plus others of my pack,
In a favourite h o s t e l r y.

Sometimes, I scavenge city
Streets, for titbits I don't need.
But I have memories
Of older times.
Then I hunt the shadows
Of wilder trails.

There is (grrrowel)
A lot of wolf, in me."

Blitz

When the sirens sang
Their mournful tune,
We ran under the stairs,

Where, protected, we felt
Almost safe.

Crouching, we listened
To the bombers sullen drone,

Feeling waves of violence
As fire bombs sought their prey.

When morning came, our fears gone
My brother and I went to play.
Blinking, amidst the steaming craters,
We harvested the shrapnel of dawn.

Whilst our parents
Tried gathering a day.

Evacuation

On a mainline London station
Fidgety little people
Left standing alone in worried clumps,
With anxious frowns.
Tied up with cardboard labels
Destination we couldn't read to know.

Arrival at some outpost far from home,
A silent row of grown-ups
Take their golden pick.
Us rest confined to local halls
For plucking out another day.
Some billeted to families
Whose choice they never were . . .

We were prisoners of childhood
And large cuckoos of war.
Urban breeds, lost in daisy fields.
A municipal saving of city kids,
Or a Jason's crop for reaping,
Another war away.

The swaying
bridge

In a wistful moment
When memory crosses your eye,
My heart pulls with yours.
The bridge of recollection
May be thrown, swaying
Over many moments in life;
Holding us, on its fine track
Balancing, precariously awhile.

Sahara winds

Sahara Winds
Come roaring down this valley,
Hazing the air,
Paling the sky,
Softening all shadows.
An edge of irritability,
Deposited, in the red dust
Of Africa.

Sirocco in
Fornalutx

A wind from Africa
Flays the valley.
With oven-gasping heat.

Carrying desert sands
In a red-brown haze
Deposited, in powerful blasts

On languishing tourists,
From colder climes.

We can not contain
Such exotic force,
And wilt beneath its lash.

The mountains
of Sóller

I want them to
Engulf me
Hold me
Absorb me.
My heart to
Become stone,
In a quite
High place:
Alone.

Sundowner

I remember an African night
Seated quietly on the veranda,
Cold beer at my side, waiting
For the sunset drama.

As the warm air flowed to dark,
The moon rose full and shiny;
So many stars lit up the sky
They spun, a great wheel round me.

I heard the sound of raucous frogs,
And mosquitoes' hungry whine.
Wild palms waved elegant fronds,
Huge Baobab trees emerged
Born again of the night.

And far away an old steam train's
Mournful whistle, crossed the great plain
Moving towards a distant rendezvous.
While my moment in time stood still.

Tears

"It will end in tears"
They often said.

And yes, it sometimes did.
But oh what joy and oh what fun

Before those tears were sprung.

Night on
Cape Maclear

Supper done, reflections due
After a glass of wine or two . . .

Waters of the lake swish,
And gurgle at our feet,
A wind-up gramophone
Crackles, straining to compete,
With far-off drums, and other
Sounds that haunt an African night.
Hissing oil lamps, pumped up
To whitest light,
Dim our circle of stars.

Beyond that line is darkness,
There are no city lights.

Fornalutx
Mallorca

It's to do with heat and silence,
And cicadas whispering songs.

Of gorgeous plants
That suck the sun
To gain exotic colour;
Gradually fading with the day
To rest, and lose all power.

But the night contains a memory,
In fragrance from their flowers.

Memories   The shades of a life gone by,

Are the reflections

Of but a moment, in the eye.

A minute of silence.

A look into space;

Encompass a lifetime

In their embrace.

Early morning

I feel lucky this morning
Waking high in the hills,
The sun near blinding me
Reflecting off Palma bay.

He sleeps . . .

We have come together
From other lives.
A little frayed at the edges.
But in reasonable nick.

He still sleeps . . .

Our pasts are alive,
And our future has hope.
I'll sing in the shower,
Though on a discordant note.

He wakes, and smiles . . .

The Woolwich
& District
Swimming
Club

On hot summer Sundays
We gathered at Danson Park
To swim in the Lido.
Young, fit, sleek porpoises
Curving the water.
Playing, laughing, diving
Falling in love, Cupid's darts
Never so strong as those flecks
Of water, gold-lit by the sun
Flying from a shaken head, or
Flicked by a playful hand.
Lazing in the heat, idle chat
Lovely boys, and girls,
Moving towards adulthood,
Helped by the sound system's blare
Of the Blue Tango.
Now I am told, a municipal decision
Was made, there are no more swimmers
Of a fine summer's day,
Just echoes of laughter.
Our pool is cemented over, closed.

Shading

All life is moving on.
There are no steps back.

Only delicate memories
Of days gone by.

And, maybe, some hopes that flew
Too high, a shading, behind the eyes.

Youth

I will never be young again,

Though the world goes on the same.

The sun warms me still.

And the winds they blow,

Perhaps a little cooler, at times.

But those fading days

Remain with me still:

Whispering, close for a while . . .

Things we
never said

I had a thought, when I came home
One day, after partying.
A little worse for wear . . .

I sat, in my summer garden,
Swallows flitting by
In the blue, cool morning air.

Suddenly, I wished that
My father was sitting
In that other chair.

So we could talk
Of things our time
Had missed before.

One drink
too many!

I am slowly and very carefully
Travelling around my day,
A hangover shadowing all the way.
Evasive action didn't do the trick.
I'll just have to work my way out of it.

The name
of love

I've thought so many loves
The first, or last.

But, in musing, I wonder,
Perhaps, they are all the same.

Because love is love,
Wherever its found.
Regardless of a name.

The A–Z

I opened my A–Z
Looking for a way.
A broad path here,
A side street there,
Goodness, a cul-de-sac.
Ho-hum, I'll turn the page.

Moving along

Once upon a time
When young,

I did not walk
In straight lines.

So my trail
Meanders somewhat.

On the road

As I turn my head, I see
A long road behind
That my youth flowed along.

Shown now, in time's gradual
Demolition of the body,
And wrinkling around an eye.

Life's teacher is still
Around though . . .
To knock me into shape;

And whispers across old fault lines,
Echoing along the way,
To linger near the future.

Olé.